Review & Remember

Social Studies Fast Facts

Written by Donna Borst, Jill Day & Mary Ellen Switzer

Illustrated by Gene Bentdahl

Presented By:

Teaching & Learning Company

1204 Buchanan St., P.O. Box 10

Carthage, IL 62321-0010

Cover design by Gene Bentdahl

Copyright © 2007, Teaching & Learning Company

ISBN No. 978-1-57310-540-8

Printing No. 987654321

Teaching & Learning Company
1204 Buchanan St., P.O. Box 10
Carthage, IL 62321-0010

Table of Contents

 Name the capital of Alabama.

 This state has the smallest population in the United States.

 The Ringling Brothers began a circus in this state.

 What is the capital of Alaska?

 The capital of Arizona is _____.

 The nickname for this state is the Mountain State.

 What is the only state to be named after a U.S. President?

 Name the capital of Arkansas.

 What is the capital of California?

 Which state is the birthplace of eight U.S. Presidents?

Wyoming

U.S. States & Capitals   Copyright © Teaching & Learning Company

Montgomery

U.S. States & Capitals   Copyright © Teaching & Learning Company

Juneau

U.S. States & Capitals   Copyright © Teaching & Learning Company

Wisconsin

U.S. States & Capitals   Copyright © Teaching & Learning Company

West Virginia

U.S. States & Capitals   Copyright © Teaching & Learning Company

Phoenix

U.S. States & Capitals   Copyright © Teaching & Learning Company

Little Rock

U.S. States & Capitals   Copyright © Teaching & Learning Company

Washington

U.S. States & Capitals   Copyright © Teaching & Learning Company

Virginia

U.S. States & Capitals   Copyright © Teaching & Learning Company

Sacramento

U.S. States & Capitals   Copyright © Teaching & Learning Company

 The capital of Colorado is _____.

 This state leads the nation in the production of maple syrup.

 The only place in the United States where four states meet.

 _____ is the capital of Connecticut.

 Name the capital of Delaware.

 What state won its independence from Mexico on April 21, 1836?

 This state is the home of the Grand Ole Opry.

 What is the capital of Florida?

 The capital of Georgia is _____.

 "Wild Bill" Hickok and Calamity Jane are buried in this state.

Vermont

U.S. States & Capitals   Copyright © Teaching & Learning Company

Denver

U.S. States & Capitals   Copyright © Teaching & Learning Company

Hartford

U.S. States & Capitals   Copyright © Teaching & Learning Company

Four Corners, Utah

U.S. States & Capitals   Copyright © Teaching & Learning Company

Texas

U.S. States & Capitals   Copyright © Teaching & Learning Company

Dover

U.S. States & Capitals   Copyright © Teaching & Learning Company

Tallahassee

U.S. States & Capitals   Copyright © Teaching & Learning Company

Tennessee

U.S. States & Capitals   Copyright © Teaching & Learning Company

South Dakota

U.S. States & Capitals   Copyright © Teaching & Learning Company

Atlanta

U.S. States & Capitals   Copyright © Teaching & Learning Company

8

 _____ is the capital of Hawaii.

 Name the first state to secede from the Union in 1860.

 Name the smallest state in the nation.

 Name the capital of Idaho.

 What is the capital of Illinois?

 The City of Brotherly Love is located in this state.

 This state leads the nation in lumber production.

 The capital of Indiana is _____.

 _____ is the capital of Iowa.

 Name two states that have panhandles.

South Carolina

Honolulu

Boise

Rhode Island

Pennsylvania

Springfield

Indianapolis

Oregon

Oklahoma, Florida and West Virginia

Des Moines

 Name the capital of Kansas.

 Name the only state that does not have a rectangular flag.

 What state marks the geographic center of North America?

 What is the capital of Kentucky?

 The capital of Louisiana is _____.

 In 1903, the Wright Brothers made the first successfully powered flight by man near Kitty Hawk, _____ .

 This state is home to the Empire State Building.

 _____ is the capital of Maine.

 Name the capital of Maryland.

 This state is home to the highest and oldest capital in the country.

Ohio

Topeka

Frankfort

North Dakota

North Carolina

Baton Rouge

Augusta

New York

New Mexico

Annapolis

 What is the capital of Massachusetts?

 The Hadrasaurus is this state's official dinosaur.

 This state has only 18 miles of coastline along the Atlantic Ocean.

 The capital of Michigan is _____.

 _____ is the capital of Minnesota.

 Wichita is the largest city in this state.

 President Abraham Lincoln was born in this state.

 Name the capital of Mississippi.

 What is the capital of Missouri?

 This state was hardest hit by Hurricane Katrina.

New Jersey

U.S. States & Capitals   Copyright © Teaching & Learning Company

Boston

U.S. States & Capitals   Copyright © Teaching & Learning Company

Lansing

U.S. States & Capitals   Copyright © Teaching & Learning Company

New Hampshire

U.S. States & Capitals   Copyright © Teaching & Learning Company

Kansas

U.S. States & Capitals   Copyright © Teaching & Learning Company

St. Paul

U.S. States & Capitals   Copyright © Teaching & Learning Company

Jackson

U.S. States & Capitals   Copyright © Teaching & Learning Company

Kentucky

U.S. States & Capitals   Copyright © Teaching & Learning Company

Louisiana

U.S. States & Capitals   Copyright © Teaching & Learning Company

Jefferson City

U.S. States & Capitals   Copyright © Teaching & Learning Company

 The capital of Montana is ____.

 New Hampshire is the only state that borders this state.

 Which state is home to the U.S. Naval Academy?

 What is the capital of Nebraska?

 The capital of Nevada is ____.

 In what state were the first shots fired in the Revolutionary War?

 The Motor City is located in this state.

 ____ is the capital of New Hampshire.

 Name the capital of New Jersey.

 One nickname for this state is Land of 10,000 Lakes.

Maine

Helena

Lincoln

Maryland

Massachusetts

Carson City

Concord

Michigan

Minnesota

Trenton

 What is the
capital of
New Mexico?

 The largest
cottonwood
plantation
can be found
in this state.

 The
Pony Express
ran from
California
to this state.

 The capital
of New York
is _____.

 _____ is the
capital of
North Carolina.

 The name
of this
state means
"mountain"
in Spanish.

 In which
state did the
Transcontinental
Railroad begin?

 Name the
capital of
North Dakota.

 What is
the capital
of Ohio?

 What state
is the nation's
leading
producer
of gold?

Mississippi

U.S. States & Capitals   Copyright © Teaching & Learning Company

Santa Fe

U.S. States & Capitals   Copyright © Teaching & Learning Company

Albany

U.S. States & Capitals   Copyright © Teaching & Learning Company

Missouri

U.S. States & Capitals   Copyright © Teaching & Learning Company

Montana

U.S. States & Capitals   Copyright © Teaching & Learning Company

Raleigh

U.S. States & Capitals   Copyright © Teaching & Learning Company

Bismarck

U.S. States & Capitals   Copyright © Teaching & Learning Company

Nebraska

U.S. States & Capitals   Copyright © Teaching & Learning Company

Nevada

U.S. States & Capitals   Copyright © Teaching & Learning Company

Columbus

U.S. States & Capitals   Copyright © Teaching & Learning Company

 The capital of Oklahoma is _____.

 This is the Grand Canyon State.

 What is the official state drink of Arkansas?

 _____ is the capital of Oregon.

 Name the capital of Pennsylvania.

 What was discovered in California in 1848?

 The capital of this state is called the Mile High City.

 What is the capital of Rhode Island?

 The capital of South Carolina is _____.

 The official song of this state is "Yankee Doodle."

Arizona

U.S. States & Capitals   Copyright © Teaching & Learning Company

Oklahoma City

U.S. States & Capitals   Copyright © Teaching & Learning Company

Salem

U.S. States & Capitals   Copyright © Teaching & Learning Company

milk

U.S. States & Capitals   Copyright © Teaching & Learning Company

gold

U.S. States & Capitals   Copyright © Teaching & Learning Company

Harrisburg

U.S. States & Capitals   Copyright © Teaching & Learning Company

Providence

U.S. States & Capitals   Copyright © Teaching & Learning Company

Colorado

U.S. States & Capitals   Copyright © Teaching & Learning Company

Connecticut

U.S. States & Capitals   Copyright © Teaching & Learning Company

Columbia

U.S. States & Capitals   Copyright © Teaching & Learning Company

 _____ is the capital of South Dakota.

 This state was the first to ratify the Constitution.

 Ponce de Leon named this state, which means "full of flowers."

 Name the capital of Tennessee.

 What is the capital of Texas?

 What state leads the nation in the production of peanuts?

 This state is made up of 132 islands.

 The capital of Utah is _____.

 _____ is the capital of Vermont.

 Name the capital of Virginia.

Delaware

Pierre

Nashville

Florida

Georgia

Austin

Salt Lake City

Hawaii

Richmond

Montpelier

 What is the capital of Washington?

 This state is bordered on the east by Montana and Wyoming.

 Illinois was the first state to ratify the _____ amendment.

 The capital of West Virginia is _____.

 _____ is the capital of Wisconsin.

 Name the capital of Wyoming.

 This state has four neighbors, including Tennessee and Florida.

 True or False? Indiana was part of the Northwest Territory.

 This state is nearly twice as big as Texas.

 The only state whose east and west borders are formed entirely by water.

Idaho

U.S. States & Capitals   Copyright © Teaching & Learning Company

Olympia

U.S. States & Capitals   Copyright © Teaching & Learning Company

Charleston

U.S. States & Capitals   Copyright © Teaching & Learning Company

13th

U.S. States & Capitals   Copyright © Teaching & Learning Company

Cheyenne

U.S. States & Capitals   Copyright © Teaching & Learning Company

Madison

U.S. States & Capitals   Copyright © Teaching & Learning Company

true

U.S. States & Capitals   Copyright © Teaching & Learning Company

Alabama

U.S. States & Capitals   Copyright © Teaching & Learning Company

Iowa

U.S. States & Capitals   Copyright © Teaching & Learning Company

Alaska

U.S. States & Capitals   Copyright © Teaching & Learning Company

 Who was the youngest man ever elected President?

 Name President Lincoln's most famous speech.

 This man was both the 22nd and 24th President.

 Who preceded Abraham Lincoln as President?

 Which President is pictured on the quarter?

 Who was President during the Panic of 1837?

 Name the President pictured on the $50 bill.

 Name the first President to use electricity in the White House.

 This President signed the law that made Texas a state in 1845.

 This President kept a paperweight on his desk that said, "The buck stops here."

Gettysburg Address

John F. Kennedy

Andrew Johnson

Grover Cleveland

Martin Van Buren

George Washington

Benjamin Harrison

Ulysses S. Grant

Harry S. Truman

John Tyler

 Name the President who was an Eagle Scout.

 President Chester A. Arthur's passage of this act was his greatest achievement.

 Which President established the Peace Corps?

 This President led the allied forces during the Normandy invasion.

 Which President's favorite treat was jelly beans?

 Name the 13th President.

 Who was President when the Civil Rights Act was passed?

 This President helped develop what is now our U.S. Treasury.

 Who was President during the Spanish-American War?

 Who was President during the Mexican War?

Pendleton Civil Service Act

U.S. Presidents　　　Copyright © Teaching & Learning Company

Gerald R. Ford

U.S. Presidents　　　Copyright © Teaching & Learning Company

Dwight D. Eisenhower

U.S. Presidents　　　Copyright © Teaching & Learning Company

John F. Kennedy

U.S. Presidents　　　Copyright © Teaching & Learning Company

Millard Fillmore

U.S. Presidents　　　Copyright © Teaching & Learning Company

Ronald Reagan

U.S. Presidents　　　Copyright © Teaching & Learning Company

Martin Van Buren

U.S. Presidents　　　Copyright © Teaching & Learning Company

Lyndon B. Johnson

U.S. Presidents　　　Copyright © Teaching & Learning Company

James K. Polk

U.S. Presidents　　　Copyright © Teaching & Learning Company

William McKinley

U.S. Presidents　　　Copyright © Teaching & Learning Company

 Name the first President to have a car.

 Which President gave the order to drop atomic bombs on Japan?

 Who was the first President to have an asteroid named after him?

 Abraham Lincoln's picture is on what coin?

 Which President pardoned President Richard M. Nixon?

 Who was President at the end of the Cold War?

 John Quincy Adams was this President's Secretary of State.

 Who was President when the Supreme Court passed the Dred Scott Decision?

 Which President was chosen commander in chief of the Continental Army?

 The President on the $20 bill is

_____.

Harry S. Truman

penny

George H.W. Bush

James Monroe

Andrew Jackson

William Howard Taft

Herbert Hoover

Gerald R. Ford

James Buchanan

George Washington

 Which President never attended school?

 This President's daughter had a candy bar (Baby Ruth™) named after her.

 Which President appointed the first woman to the Supreme Court?

 Who was the only man to become President without being elected?

 This man served 40 years as an Army officer before being elected President.

 Name the tallest President.

 Which President began the tradition of throwing out the first ball at the opening day of the baseball season?

 Which President is famous for this phrase: "Speak softly and carry a big stick."

 Name the first President to appear on television.

 Who was President when the Persian Gulf War started?

Grover Cleveland

Andrew Johnson

Gerald R. Ford

Ronald Reagan

Abraham Lincoln

Zachary Taylor

Theodore Roosevelt

William Howard Taft

George H.W. Bush

Franklin D. Roosevelt

 Who said: "Read my lips. No new taxes."

 Who was the first President to wear a beard while in office?

 Which President authorized the Louisiana Purchase?

 Which President's wife became a U.S. senator?

 Name two Presidents whose sons were also Presidents.

 Who was the first President to use a telephone in the White House?

 Who was President when the Republican Party was established?

 Who was President when 1 million square miles of territory were added to the nation?

 Who was the author of the Bill of Rights?

 Theodore Roosevelt became President when this President was assassinated.

Abraham Lincoln

George H.W. Bush

William J. Clinton

Thomas Jefferson

Rutherford B. Hayes

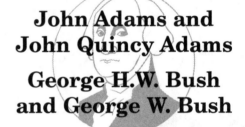

**John Adams and
John Quincy Adams**

**George H.W. Bush
and George W. Bush**

James K. Polk

Franklin Pierce

William McKinley

James Madison

 Which President is pictured on the $5 bill?

 Which two men signed the Declaration of Independence and later became Presidents?

 This President enacted the nation's first income tax.

 Which President was well-known for being a peanut farmer?

 Who served the most years as President?

 Which President was a famous Hollywood actor?

 Name the first President sworn into office by a woman.

 Which President named his son George Washington?

 This man lost the 1960 presidential election to John F. Kennedy.

 Name the first President to be a Rhodes scholar.

John Adams,
Thomas Jefferson

U.S. Presidents   Copyright © Teaching & Learning Company

Abraham Lincoln

U.S. Presidents   Copyright © Teaching & Learning Company

Jimmy Carter

U.S. Presidents   Copyright © Teaching & Learning Company

Woodrow Wilson

U.S. Presidents   Copyright © Teaching & Learning Company

Ronald Reagan

U.S. Presidents   Copyright © Teaching & Learning Company

Franklin D. Roosevelt

U.S. Presidents   Copyright © Teaching & Learning Company

John Quincy Adams

U.S. Presidents   Copyright © Teaching & Learning Company

Lyndon B. Johnson

U.S. Presidents   Copyright © Teaching & Learning Company

William J. Clinton

U.S. Presidents   Copyright © Teaching & Learning Company

Richard M. Nixon

U.S. Presidents   Copyright © Teaching & Learning Company

 Who was President when the nation was 100 years old?

 This President established the first permanent library in the White House.

 What two Presidents died on July 4th?

 Which President had twin daughters?

 Name the President whose picture is on the dime.

 Who was the only President to resign from office?

 Who was the first man from Arkansas to be elected President?

 Who was President at the beginning of the War of 1812?

 Who was the shortest President?

 The President from 1853-1857 was

_____.

Millard Fillmore

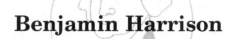

Benjamin Harrison

George W. Bush

John Adams,
Thomas Jefferson

Richard M. Nixon

Franklin D. Roosevelt

James Madison

William J. Clinton

Franklin Pierce

James Madison

 Who was the first Secretary of State?

 Who was President when the Stock Market crashed in October 1929?

 Which President served the shortest term in office?

 Which President is pictured on the $1 bill?

 Name the second President to be assassinated.

 Which President was appointed Chief Justice of the Supreme Court?

 The Teapot Dome Scandal took place during which President's administration?

 Which President held the first televised news conference? (He was also the first President to be televised in color.)

 Name the President who appointed the first African-American to the Supreme Court.

 Name the three Presidents who have received a Nobel Prize.

Herbert Hoover

Thomas Jefferson

George Washington

William Henry Harrison

William Howard Taft

James A. Garfield

Dwight D. Eisenhower

Warren G. Harding

Theodore Roosevelt, Woodrow Wilson, Jimmy Carter

Lyndon B. Johnson

 Who said: "Ask not what your country can do for you. Ask what you can do for your country."

 Who was the first Vice President to take office after the death of the President?

 Name the first President to travel outside of the United States.

 Name the first President who donated his presidential salary to charity.

 Who was known as "Old Rough and Ready"?

 Who was the only President to fight in both the Revolutionary War and the War of 1812?

 Who was President when Alaska and Hawaii became part of the United States?

 Thomas Jefferson's picture is on what coin?

 Which President made Yellowstone the nation's first national park?

 Who said: "I do not choose to run for President in 1928."

John Tyler

U.S. Presidents Copyright © Teaching & Learning Company

John F. Kennedy

U.S. Presidents Copyright © Teaching & Learning Company

Herbert Hoover

U.S. Presidents Copyright © Teaching & Learning Company

Theodore Roosevelt

U.S. Presidents Copyright © Teaching & Learning Company

Andrew Jackson

U.S. Presidents Copyright © Teaching & Learning Company

Zachary Taylor

U.S. Presidents Copyright © Teaching & Learning Company

nickel

U.S. Presidents Copyright © Teaching & Learning Company

Dwight D. Eisenhower

U.S. Presidents Copyright © Teaching & Learning Company

Calvin Coolidge

U.S. Presidents Copyright © Teaching & Learning Company

Ulysses S. Grant

U.S. Presidents Copyright © Teaching & Learning Company

 This President's grandson became the 23rd President.

 Which President is pictured on the 50¢ (half-dollar) coin?

 Which President is known for ending Reconstruction?

 Name the first President to have a radio in the White House.

 Which President said: "The only thing we have to fear is fear itself."

 What policy is James Monroe best known for?

 Name the first President to visit the U.S.S.R.

 The only President to never marry was

_____.

 Who was the first President born in a hospital?

 Who was the oldest person ever to be elected President?

John F. Kennedy

William Henry Harrison

Warren G. Harding

Rutherford B. Hayes

The Monroe Doctrine

Franklin D. Roosevelt

James Buchanan

Richard M. Nixon

Ronald Reagan

Jimmy Carter

 The first 10 amendments to the U.S. Constitution are called the _____.

 How many senators does each state have?

 This scandal led to the resignation of President Richard M. Nixon.

 In what year did women get the right to vote?

 This was considered the doorway through the Rocky Mountains for the emigrants on the Oregon Trail.

 The term for a U.S. senator is how many years?

 What caused the Mississippi to run backward?

 During World War II, these Marines transmitted vital communications that were undecipherable to the enemy.

 Alexander Hamilton formed this party to oppose the Democratic-Republicans.

 Name three of the original 13 colonies.

2

Bill of Rights

1920

Watergate

6 years

South Pass

Navajo Code Breakers

New Madrid earthquake

Connecticut, Delaware, Georgia, Maine, Maryland, Massachusetts, New Hampshire, New Jersey, New York, Pennsylvania, Rhode Island, Vermont, Virginia

Federalist Party

 This act, imposed by the British in 1767, taxed imports such as paint and lead into the colonies.

 The leader of the U.S. House of Representatives is called

_____.

 This event took place on December 7, 1941.

 This is where General Lee surrendered to General Grant to end the Civil War.

 Paul Revere made his famous ride in what year?

 President Johnson signed this in 1964 to prohibit discrimination of all kinds.

 During the Great Depression, President Franklin D. Roosevelt initiated this to provide "relief, recovery and reform."

 Which American colony was *not* represented in the First Continental Congress?

 In 1945, the United States dropped an atomic bomb on these two cities.

 Which state was the site of the Battle of Little Big Horn?

Speaker of the House

Townshend Acts

Appomattox

Japan attacked Pearl Harbor.

Civil Rights Act

1775

Georgia

New Deal

Montana

Hiroshima and Nagasaki, Japan

 Who has the power to declare war?

 How many years is a United States President's term?

 Which British general surrendered to George Washington at Yorktown?

 In 1808, John Colter stumbled upon land where hot water shot straight into the air. Today, this place is called _____.

 Each year the President is required to give this speech in January.

 What were greenbacks?

 A severe drought during the 1930s caused this.

 The British burned this major city in 1814, destroying many landmark buildings.

 What major city was part of the Louisiana Purchase?

 Who is the commander in chief of the U.S. Army and Navy?

4 years

Congress

Yellowstone National Park

General Cornwallis

first paper currency authorized by the U.S. Congress

State of the Union Address

Washington, D.C.

Dust Bowl

President

New Orleans

 Which President is known for delivering the Four Freedoms Speech?

 What was the purpose of the women's suffrage movement?

 The Treaty of Versailles ended this war.

 How many years is a U.S. representative's term?

 This war divided the nation into the North and the South.

 The Declaration of Independence was signed on what date?

 World War I began in 1917 when the United States declared war on this country.

 Name the first permanent English settlement in America.

 In 1860, mail was delivered between Missouri and California by riders on horses known as the _____.

 In what year did World War II end?

to win the right to vote

American History   Copyright © Teaching & Learning Company

Franklin D. Roosevelt

American History   Copyright © Teaching & Learning Company

2 years

American History   Copyright © Teaching & Learning Company

World War I

American History   Copyright © Teaching & Learning Company

July 4, 1776

American History   Copyright © Teaching & Learning Company

Civil War

American History   Copyright © Teaching & Learning Company

Jamestown

American History   Copyright © Teaching & Learning Company

Germany

American History   Copyright © Teaching & Learning Company

1945

American History   Copyright © Teaching & Learning Company

Pony Express

American History   Copyright © Teaching & Learning Company

 In what year did the first Continental Congress meet?

 The number of electors each state has is based on what?

 The Cold War was between the United States and this country.

 Over 55 million acres of the United States are used for this.

 This governing document was drafted by the Pilgrims in 1620.

 What did the three colors on the first U.S. flag represent?

 Who appoints Supreme Court justices?

 What event happened on November 22, 1963?

 Lewis and Clark began their famous expedition in this city.

 In 1838, thousands of Cherokee Indians were forced from their homes in Georgia and sent to Oklahoma along this route.

number of senators plus number of representatives

1774

Indian reservations

Soviet Union

**white purity
red valor
blue perseverance and jus tice**

Mayflower Compact

assassination of President John F. Kennedy

President

Trail of Tears

St. Louis, Missouri

 What act taxed most colonial paper goods (newspapers, pamphlets, books, playing cards and all legal documents)?

 The largest earthquake ever recorded in the contiguous United States occurred in this state in 1812.

 This group of people, ancestors of the present-day Pueblo Indians, carved their homes on rock ledges.

 For how many terms can a President be elected?

 The District of Columbia was given to the government by what two states?

 The first Thanksgiving was celebrated here in 1621.

 How many stars and stripes did the first U.S. flag have?

 General George Custer lost his life in this battle with the Sioux.

 This loosely organized system helped fugitive slaves escape to areas of safety.

 From what country did the Pilgrims leave to come to America?

Missouri

Stamp Act

2

Cliff Dwellers

Plymouth Colony

Virginia and Maryland

Battle of Little Big Horn

13 stars and 13 stripes

England

Underground Railroad

 What is the name of our country's national anthem?

 How many branches are in the U.S. government?

 The legislative branch of the government consists of

_____.

 This event in 1890 is considered the last major battle between white soldiers and Native Americans.

 In what year did "The Star-Spangled Banner" become the official national anthem?

 Why was everyone watching television on July 20, 1969?

 The Pilgrims came to America searching for

_____

freedom.

 What famous speech starts with this phrase: "Four score and seven years ago . . ."

 The head judge on the Supreme Court holds this title.

 Who founded the Library of Congress?

3

The Star-Spangled Banner

Wounded Knee Massacre

Congress

Neil Armstrong was walking on the moon.

1931

Abraham Lincoln s Gettysburg Address

religious

Thomas Jefferson

Chief Justice

 This decision by the Supreme Court made segregation in schools illegal.

 The Boston Tea Party took place in what year?

 In the original Constitution, how many articles were there?

 If both the President and Vice President are incapacitated, who takes over?

 What two words were added to the Pledge of Allegiance in 1954?

 In what year did the Stamp Act take place?

 What famous island operated as an immigration center from 1892-1943?

 The first transcontinental railroad was built between these two cities.

 What year was the nation's first President sworn into office?

 What determines the number of representatives a state receives?

1773

Brown vs. Board of Education

Speaker of the House

7

1765

under God

Sacramento, California, and Omaha, Nebraska

Ellis Island

population

1789

 What did James Marshall discover at Sutter's Mill in 1848?

 This noteworthy sentence begins with "We the people . . . :"

 Name the capital of the United States.

 The executive branch of the government consists of _____.

 Desert Storm was a U.S. military operation during this war.

 The final draft of the Emancipation Proclamation was issued in what year?

 The highest court in the U.S. judicial system is called the _____.

 Where was the "shot heard 'round the world" fired?

 In what year did the Supreme Court meet for the first time?

 In 1620, this ship brought Pilgrims seeking freedom of worship to Cape Cod.

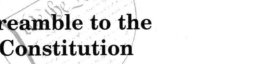

Preamble to the Constitution

gold

the President

Washington, D.C.

1863

Persian Gulf War

Lexington-Concord

Supreme Court

Mayflower

1790

 What are the President's chief advisors called?

 The judicial branch of the government consists of

_____.

 The first telephone message was sent during this year.

 This space shuttle exploded just 73 seconds after liftoff.

 What was the name of the poem that later became "The Star-Spangled Banner"?

 What happened on Black Thursday in 1929?

 This executive order abolished slavery in the Confederate states.

 How many judges are on the Supreme Court?

 Which amendment to the Constitution outlawed slavery?

 What treaty formally ended the Revolutionary War?

the Supreme Court and the lower federal courts

American History · Copyright © Teaching & Learning Company

Cabinet

American History · Copyright © Teaching & Learning Company

Challenger

American History · Copyright © Teaching & Learning Company

1876

American History · Copyright © Teaching & Learning Company

Stock Market crashed

American History · Copyright © Teaching & Learning Company

The Defense of Fort McHenry

American History · Copyright © Teaching & Learning Company

9

American History · Copyright © Teaching & Learning Company

Emancipation Proclamation

American History · Copyright © Teaching & Learning Company

Treaty of Paris

American History · Copyright © Teaching & Learning Company

13th Amendment

American History · Copyright © Teaching & Learning Company

TLC10540 Copyright © Teaching & Learning Company, Carthage, IL 62321

 What was the
name of the
first U.S.
Supreme Court
Chief Justice?

 Some
considered this
man America's
first political
cartoonist.

 He developed
hundreds of new
uses for peanuts,
sweet potatoes
and other crops
at Alabama's
Tuskegee Institute.

 Name the first
African-American
woman to sing at
the Metropolitan
Opera House.

 This man was
the first to sign
the Declaration
of Independence.
He also had the
largest signature
on the document.

 Who wrote the
poem "America
the Beautiful,"
which later
became a song?

 In 1927,
who made the
first flight
across the
Atlantic Ocean?

 Name the
first man to
reach the
North Pole.

 This man
invented
the electric
light and
many other
inventions.

 She was
the first
American
woman to go
into space.

Benjamin Franklin

Famous Americans   Copyright © Teaching & Learning Company

John Jay

Famous Americans   Copyright © Teaching & Learning Company

Marian Anderson

Famous Americans   Copyright © Teaching & Learning Company

George Washington Carver

Famous Americans   Copyright © Teaching & Learning Company

Katharine Lee Bates

Famous Americans   Copyright © Teaching & Learning Company

John Hancock

Famous Americans   Copyright © Teaching & Learning Company

Robert Edwin Peary

Famous Americans   Copyright © Teaching & Learning Company

Charles Lindbergh

Famous Americans   Copyright © Teaching & Learning Company

Sally Ride

Famous Americans   Copyright © Teaching & Learning Company

Thomas Edison

Famous Americans   Copyright © Teaching & Learning Company

 She wrote an amendment in 1878, which later became the 19th Amendment giving women the right to vote.

 These brothers were the first to fly a controlled plane over a distance.

 In 1908, he introduced the Model T.

 The Battle at Little Big Horn was his last stand.

 This legendary lawman was shot and killed in 1876 while playing poker in Deadwood, South Dakota.

 This woman started Hull House in 1889.

 This African-American studied astronomy, built the first American clock and helped plan our nation's capital.

 This Indian was a Sioux chief who played a large part in defeating Custer's army at Little Big Horn.

 Along with Susan B. Anthony, this woman formed the National Woman Suffrage Association.

 His pen name was Mark Twain.

Wilbur and Orville Wright

Susan B. Anthony

Lt. Col. George Custer

Henry Ford

Jane Addams

Wild Bill Hickok

Sitting Bull

Benjamin Banneker

Samuel Clemens

Elizabeth Cady Stanton

 This woman organized the first American Red Cross.

 He was the president of the Confederate States of America.

 His best-known invention was the cotton gin.

 This man's first dictionary took 27 years to complete.

 This man was the first to walk on the moon.

 This author is best known for writing *Little Women*.

 This U.S. senator was an extreme anti-communist in the 1950s.

 This Apache chief was involved in The Bascom Affair, which triggered the Apache Wars.

 This American pioneer is best known for his exploration and settlement of what is now Kentucky.

 He holds the distinction of being the first American to travel into space.

Jefferson Davis

Famous Americans   Copyright © Teaching & Learning Company

Clara Barton

Famous Americans   Copyright © Teaching & Learning Company

Noah Webster

Famous Americans   Copyright © Teaching & Learning Company

Eli Whitney

Famous Americans   Copyright © Teaching & Learning Company

Louisa May Alcott

Famous Americans   Copyright © Teaching & Learning Company

Neil Armstrong

Famous Americans   Copyright © Teaching & Learning Company

Cochise

Famous Americans   Copyright © Teaching & Learning Company

Joseph McCarthy

Famous Americans   Copyright © Teaching & Learning Company

Alan Shepard, Jr.

Famous Americans   Copyright © Teaching & Learning Company

Daniel Boone

Famous Americans   Copyright © Teaching & Learning Company

 This woman accompanied Lewis and Clark on their journey and served as a guide and translator.

 This Confederate general is best known by the nickname he got during the First Battle of Bull Run.

 This heroine from the American Revolution earned her nickname by carrying water to soldiers during battle.

 This woman is thought to have sewn the first American flag in 1776.

 This man took a famous ride on April 18, 1775.

 Born into slavery, this man eventually became one of America's most productive abolitionists.

 Once an American military hero during the Revolutionary War, this man is best known as a traitor to the United States.

 In 1846, he invented the first American-patented sewing machine.

 This man's lifesaving maneuver has saved hundreds of choking victims.

 She was the first woman justice to serve on the Supreme Court.

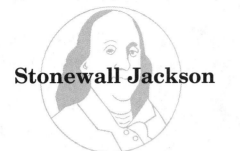

Stonewall Jackson

Famous Americans   Copyright © Teaching & Learning Company

Sacagawea

Famous Americans   Copyright © Teaching & Learning Company

Betsy Ross

Famous Americans   Copyright © Teaching & Learning Company

Molly Pitcher

Famous Americans   Copyright © Teaching & Learning Company

Frederick Douglass

Famous Americans   Copyright © Teaching & Learning Company

Paul Revere

Famous Americans   Copyright © Teaching & Learning Company

Elias Howe

Famous Americans   Copyright © Teaching & Learning Company

Benedict Arnold

Famous Americans   Copyright © Teaching & Learning Company

Sandra Day O Connor

Famous Americans   Copyright © Teaching & Learning Company

Henry Heimlich

Famous Americans   Copyright © Teaching & Learning Company

 He developed the vaccine for polio.

 John Chapman has become an American legend better known by this nickname.

 This author's real name is Theodor S. Geisel.

 We can thank this man for animated classics such as *Dumbo, Bambi* and *Snow White.*

 Maya Lin was the artist chosen to design this Washington, D.C., landmark.

 This man wrote the poem that eventually became America's national anthem.

 This artist was famous for his *Saturday Evening Post* covers.

 She began writing the classic *Little House* books in 1932.

 This renowned American folk artist didn't begin painting until she was in her 70s.

 This man has the distinction of being the first African-American in space.

Johnny Appleseed

Dr. Jonas Salk

Walt Disney

Dr. Seuss

Francis Scott Key

Vietnam Veterans Memorial Wall

Laura Ingalls Wilder

Norman Rockwell

Guion S. Bluford, Jr.

Grandma Moses

 She was the first woman to fly solo across the Atlantic Ocean.

 She founded the Girl Scouts of the U.S.A. on March 12, 1912, in Savannah, Georgia.

 Along with his brother Frank, this man is considered to be one of the most notorious outlaws of the 1800s.

 Born in 1802, this woman worked tirelessly for humane treatment of the mentally ill.

 He wrote "The Stars and Stripes Forever," which is the national march of the United States.

 Born into slavery, this women's rights activist is remembered for her "Ain't I a Woman" speech, delivered in 1851.

 He is thought to be the most celebrated general of the Confederate Army and was the senior military advisor to Jefferson Davis.

 This American folk hero from Tennessee died at the Alamo.

 He was the first African-American Supreme Court justice.

 She wrote "The Battle Hymn of the Republic."

Juliette Gordon Lowe

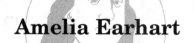

Amelia Earhart

Dorothea Dix

Jesse James

Sojourner Truth

John Philip Sousa

Davy Crockett

Robert E. Lee

Julia Ward Howe

Thurgood Marshall

 She was the first First Lady to live in the White House.

 After refusing to give up her seat on a city bus, this woman became the "Mother of the Civil Rights Movement."

 His "I Have a Dream" speech is credited with prompting the 1964 Civil Rights Act.

 As a runaway slave herself, this woman eventually led hundreds of slaves to freedom along the Underground Railroad.

 Who said: "I only regret that I have but one life to lose for my country."

 This Native-American girl was a frequent visitor to Jamestown.

 *Stopping by Woods on a Snowy Evening* is one of this poet's most famous works.

 This author likes to write about "Fudge."

 Although this man was a prominent figure in the American Revolution, he is primarily remembered for his "Give Me Liberty, or Give Me Death" speech.

 Many of this African-American author's writings focused on slavery, including *Uncle Tom's Cabin*.

Rosa Parks

Famous Americans   Copyright © Teaching & Learning Company

Abigail Adams

Famous Americans   Copyright © Teaching & Learning Company

Harriet Tubman

Famous Americans   Copyright © Teaching & Learning Company

Martin Luther King, Jr.

Famous Americans   Copyright © Teaching & Learning Company

Pocahontas

Famous Americans   Copyright © Teaching & Learning Company

Nathan Hale

Famous Americans   Copyright © Teaching & Learning Company

Judy Blume

Famous Americans   Copyright © Teaching & Learning Company

Robert Frost

Famous Americans   Copyright © Teaching & Learning Company

Harriet Beecher Stowe

Famous Americans   Copyright © Teaching & Learning Company

Patrick Henry

Famous Americans   Copyright © Teaching & Learning Company

 She became the first deaf-blind person to graduate from college.

 His best-selling autobiography was titled *Up from Slavery*.

 As America's most famous naturalist, he was often called "The Father of Our National Parks."

 This Native-American helped the Pilgrims at Plymouth Colony by teaching them how to fish and plant corn.

 She started her own school for African-American girls in 1904.

 He invented the telegraph, which included a dot-and-dash code.

 He founded Microsoft® and developed the computer program Windows®.

 Chosen to be the first teacher in space, she died when the *Challenger* exploded in 1986.

 He was the first American to orbit Earth.

 He killed Alexander Hamilton in the most famous duel in American history.

Booker T. Washington

Famous Americans   Copyright © Teaching & Learning Company

Helen Keller

Famous Americans   Copyright © Teaching & Learning Company

Squanto

Famous Americans   Copyright © Teaching & Learning Company

John Muir

Famous Americans   Copyright © Teaching & Learning Company

Samuel F.B. Morse

Famous Americans   Copyright © Teaching & Learning Company

Mary McLeod Bethune

Famous Americans   Copyright © Teaching & Learning Company

Christa McAuliffe

Famous Americans   Copyright © Teaching & Learning Company

Bill Gates

Famous Americans   Copyright © Teaching & Learning Company

Aaron Burr

Famous Americans   Copyright © Teaching & Learning Company

John Glenn

Famous Americans   Copyright © Teaching & Learning Company

 Before starting his Wild West Show, he was a scout and hunter for the army.

 She was the first known American woman to impersonate a man in order to join the army.

 President George Washington appointed him the first Secretary of the Treasury.

 She wrote her first poem at age 14 and later became the first African-American female writer to be published in the country.

 This legendary markswoman won many awards in "Buffalo Bill's" Wild West Show.

 This notorious outlaw couple traveled the Midwest during the Great Depression.

 He is most famous for the patent of the telephone.

 This "lady of the lamp" was a pioneer of modern nursing.

 These two men led the Corps of Discovery on an expedition to the Pacific Ocean and back.

 This author is probably best known for *Charlotte's Web*.

Deborah Sampson

Buffalo Bill Cody

Famous Americans   Copyright © Teaching & Learning Company

Famous Americans   Copyright © Teaching & Learning Company

Phillis Wheatley

Alexander Hamilton

Famous Americans   Copyright © Teaching & Learning Company

Famous Americans   Copyright © Teaching & Learning Company

Bonnie Parker
and
Clyde Barrow

Annie Oakley

Famous Americans   Copyright © Teaching & Learning Company

Famous Americans   Copyright © Teaching & Learning Company

Florence Nightingale

Alexander Graham Bell

Famous Americans   Copyright © Teaching & Learning Company

Famous Americans   Copyright © Teaching & Learning Company

E.B. White

Meriwether Lewis
and
William Clark

Famous Americans   Copyright © Teaching & Learning Company

Famous Americans   Copyright © Teaching & Learning Company

 She was the first African-American woman elected to Congress.

 This American zoologist dedicated her life to saving gorillas and their habitats.

 He developed the Cherokee alphabet, which allowed thousands of Native Americans to become literate.

 This "Father of the American Navy" is remembered for his battle cry: "I have not yet begun to fight."

 This famous cellist's name sounds like a children's toy.

 Some of this author's favorite characters are Ramona, Henry and Ralph S. Mouse.

 He is considered America's most famous architect.

 This man founded the company known for its green and yellow tractors.

 This author's book, *Holes,* won the Newbery Medal in 1999.

 This man is credited with designing the first artificial heart.

Dian Fossey

Famous Americans   Copyright © Teaching & Learning Company

Shirley Chisholm

Famous Americans   Copyright © Teaching & Learning Company

John Paul Jones

Famous Americans   Copyright © Teaching & Learning Company

Sequoyah

Famous Americans   Copyright © Teaching & Learning Company

Beverly Cleary

Famous Americans   Copyright © Teaching & Learning Company

Yo-Yo Ma

Famous Americans   Copyright © Teaching & Learning Company

John Deere

Famous Americans   Copyright © Teaching & Learning Company

Frank Lloyd Wright

Famous Americans   Copyright © Teaching & Learning Company

Dr. Robert Jarvik

Famous Americans   Copyright © Teaching & Learning Company

Louis Sachar

Famous Americans   Copyright © Teaching & Learning Company

 True or False?
The popular
tourist attraction
Niagara Falls
is the tallest
waterfall in
the world.

 What river
provides the
water for
Niagara Falls?

 Name the
second-largest
mountain
range in North
America.

 True or False?
The Appalachian
Mountains stretch
from Canada
to Alabama.

 Why are
the White
Mountains in
New Hampshire
called the
"Presidential
Range"?

 True or False?
Tourists who want
to visit Cape Cod
National Seashore
should head to the
state of Maine.

 The Long Trail
is the oldest
long-distance
hiking trail in the
United States.
What state is it
in: Vermont or
Connecticut?

 The famous
Finger Lakes
are located in
what state?

 The largest
estuary in the
United States
is the
_____ Bay.

 The
Chesapeake Bay
divides what
state into
two parts?

Niagara River

false

true

Appalachian Mountains

**False: It's in the
state of Massachusetts.**

**Some of the peaks are
named after U.S. Presidents.**

New York

Vermont

Maryland

Chesapeake

 The Statue of Liberty National Monument stands on what island in New York harbor?

 The Statue of Libery was given to the United States by what country?

 The outside of the Statue of Liberty is made of _____.

 How many spikes does the Statue of Liberty's crown have?

 How many windows are in the Statue of Liberty's crown: 25 or 30?

 True or False? The U.S. Military Academy at West Point is located in the state of Connecticut.

 This museum in Cooperstown, New York, features information and exhibits about the game of baseball.

 The Empire State Building is located in what city?

 This New Hampshire planetarium was named after the teacher who died in the *Challenger* space shuttle explosion.

 Name the nation's oldest suspension bridge, which was built in Newburyport, Massachusetts.

France

Geography   Copyright © Teaching & Learning Company

Liberty Island

Geography   Copyright © Teaching & Learning Company

7 spikes

Geography   Copyright © Teaching & Learning Company

copper

Geography   Copyright © Teaching & Learning Company

**False:
It is located in New York.**

Geography   Copyright © Teaching & Learning Company

25 windows

Geography   Copyright © Teaching & Learning Company

New York City

Geography   Copyright © Teaching & Learning Company

**National Baseball
Hall of Fame and Museum**

Geography   Copyright © Teaching & Learning Company

Chain Bridge

Geography   Copyright © Teaching & Learning Company

**Christa McAuliffe
Planetarium**

Geography   Copyright © Teaching & Learning Company

TLC10540 Copyright © Teaching & Learning Company, Carthage, IL 62321-0

 The Chesapeake Bay opens to what ocean?

 The Blue Ridge Mountains are part of what large mountain range: the Appalachian or Rocky Mountains?

 Shenandoah National Park in the Blue Ridge Mountains is located in what state?

 What state is nicknamed the "Mountain State" because of its many hills and mountains: Virginia or West Virginia?

 The Outer Banks of North Carolina are a long string of barrier _____ that lie offshore.

 Cape Hatteras National Seashore, the first national United States seashore, is in which state?

 Name the nation's largest freshwater swamp, which is located in Georgia and Florida.

 Florida is sometimes called the "Peninsula State" because it is surrounded by _____ on three sides.

 This well-known national park in Florida has been called the country's largest subtropical wilderness.

 What large reptile is often called the "King of the Everglades"?

Appalachian Mountains

Geography   Copyright © Teaching & Learning Company

Atlantic Ocean

Geography   Copyright © Teaching & Learning Company

West Virginia

Geography   Copyright © Teaching & Learning Company

Virginia

Geography   Copyright © Teaching & Learning Company

North Carolina

Geography   Copyright © Teaching & Learning Company

islands

Geography   Copyright © Teaching & Learning Company

water

Geography   Copyright © Teaching & Learning Company

Okefenokee Swamp

Geography   Copyright © Teaching & Learning Company

American alligator

Geography   Copyright © Teaching & Learning Company

Everglades National Park

Geography   Copyright © Teaching & Learning Company

The historic symbol of freedom known as the Liberty Bell is found in what city?

The Liberty Bell in Philadelphia was rung on July 8, 1776, to celebrate the signing of what document?

The Liberty Bell was originally cast in what country?

Dinosaur National Monument is located in this state.

This building in Philadelphia is where both the Declaration of Independence and the U.S. Constitution were created.

This zoo, the oldest in the nation, was founded in 1859.

This Pennsylvania town got its name from a large chocolate factory there.

The U.S. _____ Academy is located in Annapolis, Maryland.

The National Mall is a large park in Washington, D.C., that extends from the U.S. capitol to what river?

The Washington Monument honors what American President?

Declaration of Independence

Geography   Copyright © Teaching & Learning Company

Philadelphia, Pennsylvania

Geography   Copyright © Teaching & Learning Company

Colorado

Geography   Copyright © Teaching & Learning Company

England

Geography   Copyright © Teaching & Learning Company

Philadelphia Zoo

Geography   Copyright © Teaching & Learning Company

Independence Hall

Geography   Copyright © Teaching & Learning Company

Naval

Geography   Copyright © Teaching & Learning Company

Hershey, Pennsylvania

Geography   Copyright © Teaching & Learning Company

George Washington

Geography   Copyright © Teaching & Learning Company

Potomac River

Geography   Copyright © Teaching & Learning Company

 The world's largest population of manatees lives in what state?

 What is the main threat to the Florida manatees?

 The Florida Keys is a chain of small _____.

 Which state is home to the Mammoth Cave System, the longest cave system in the world: Kentucky or Tennessee?

 Name the nation's largest manmade lake, which is located in Nevada.

 Name the state that is home to the Lost Sea, called the world's largest underground lake.

 _____ Falls in Tennessee is the nation's highest underground waterfall.

 Ancient Stone Age artifacts have been uncovered in Russell Cave in what state: Mississippi or Alabama?

 The nation's only active diamond mine is the Crater of _____ State Park in Arkansas.

 What state is sometimes called the "Hot Springs State"?

**being struck by boats
or cut by propellers**

Geography   Copyright © Teaching & Learning Company

Florida

Geography   Copyright © Teaching & Learning Company

Kentucky

Geography   Copyright © Teaching & Learning Company

islands

Geography   Copyright © Teaching & Learning Company

Tennessee

Geography   Copyright © Teaching & Learning Company

Lake Meade

Geography   Copyright © Teaching & Learning Company

Alabama

Geography   Copyright © Teaching & Learning Company

Ruby

Geography   Copyright © Teaching & Learning Company

Arkansas

Geography   Copyright © Teaching & Learning Company

Diamonds

Geography   Copyright © Teaching & Learning Company

 What is the shape of the Washington Monument?

 This well-known landmark was built in Washington, D.C., in honor of Abraham Lincoln.

 What famous speech is carved in the walls of the Lincoln Memorial?

 Name the historic building in Washington, D.C., that houses the United States Congress.

 What is the name of the bronze statue that tops the Capitol building dome in Washington, D.C.?

 The official residence of the President of the United States is the White House. What is its address?

 What is the presidential office at the White House called?

 The first U.S. President to live in the White House was _____.

 Name the world's largest museum, which is located in Washington, D.C.

 In which cemetery is the Tomb of the Unknowns located?

Lincoln Memorial

Geography   Copyright © Teaching & Learning Company

obelisk

Geography   Copyright © Teaching & Learning Company

Capitol

Geography   Copyright © Teaching & Learning Company

Gettysburg Address

Geography   Copyright © Teaching & Learning Company

1600 Pennsylvania Avenue Washington, D.C.

Geography   Copyright © Teaching & Learning Company

Statue of Freedom

Geography   Copyright © Teaching & Learning Company

John Adams

Geography   Copyright © Teaching & Learning Company

Oval Office

Geography   Copyright © Teaching & Learning Company

Arlington National Cemetery

Geography   Copyright © Teaching & Learning Company

Smithsonian Institution

Geography   Copyright © Teaching & Learning Company

 Louisiana is bordered by the Gulf of _____ on the south.

 Name the five Great Lakes.

 True or False? The Great Lakes are filled with salt water.

 Name the largest of the five Great Lakes.

 Four of the five Great Lakes border what state?

 True or False? The smallest of the five Great Lakes is Lake Superior.

 Mackinac Island is located in which of the Great Lakes: Lake Erie or Lake Huron?

 The Chicago River in Illinois is dyed green on what holiday?

 The Mississippi River starts in which state: Wisconsin or Minnesota?

 A popular nickname for the Mississippi River is "Old _____ River."

**Lake Huron,
Lake Ontario, Lake Michigan,
Lake Erie, Lake Superior**

Geography

Mexico

Geography

Lake Superior

Geography

**False: They are
filled with fresh water.**

Geography

**False: The smallest
is Lake Ontario.**

Geography

Michigan

Geography

St. Patrick's Day

Geography

Lake Huron

Geography

Man

Geography

Minnesota

Geography

 Arlington National Cemetery is located on the _____ River.

 This five-sided building in Arlington, Virginia, is the nation's largest office building.

 What is the name of George Washington's home, which is located in Virginia?

 Which President designed his own home in Virginia named Monticello?

 This photography artist is well known for his black and white landscape photos of national parks.

 True or False? The famous Biltmore Estate in Asheville is located in Virginia.

 Cape Hatteras Lighthouse is the name of the tallest brick lighthouse (208 feet tall) in America. In what state is it located?

 The figures of Robert E. Lee, "Stonewall" Jackson, and Jefferson Davis are carved in _____ Mountain located in the state of Georgia.

 "Peachoid" is a giant water _____ built in South Carolina as a tribute to the state's peach crops.

 U.S. space shuttles are launched at this Florida space center.

Pentagon

Potomac

Thomas Jefferson

Mount Vernon

false

Ansel Adams

Stone

North Carolina

Kennedy Space Center

tower

 The nation's lowest point, at 282 feet below sea level, is located in _____, California.

 What state is sometimes called the "Cave State" because it has over 5500 caves?

 Tourists who want to visit the Badlands, Wind Cave National Park and Mount Rushmore should head to what state?

 True or False? Wind Cave National Park in South Dakota was the first cave to be designated a national park.

 Name the 500-foot rock in Nebraska that marked the beginning of the West for pioneers traveling the Oregon Trail.

 What state is nicknamed the "Sunflower State"?

 Padre Island, the longest remaining undeveloped barrier island in the nation, is located in what state: Texas or Louisiana?

 Big Bend National Park in Texas borders what river: the Red River or the Rio Grande River?

 What state is nicknamed the "Treasure State" because of its many mines: Montana or Idaho?

 What state is home to Glacier National Park?

Missouri

Geography Copyright © Teaching & Learning Company

Death Valley

Geography Copyright © Teaching & Learning Company

true

Geography Copyright © Teaching & Learning Company

South Dakota

Geography Copyright © Teaching & Learning Company

Kansas

Geography Copyright © Teaching & Learning Company

Chimney Rock

Geography Copyright © Teaching & Learning Company

Rio Grande River

Geography Copyright © Teaching & Learning Company

Texas

Geography Copyright © Teaching & Learning Company

Montana

Geography Copyright © Teaching & Learning Company

Montana

Geography Copyright © Teaching & Learning Company

 Alligator Alley is the east-west road that crosses South Florida through what large well-known marshland?

 Disney World is located in what state?

 The Mackinac Bridge (Mighty Mac) connects the upper and lower peninsulas of what state?

 Tourists who want to visit the Pro Football Hall of Fame should visit what city and state?

 The popular "Indy 500" car race is held every year at this Indiana speedway.

 The nation's tallest building is the _____ in Chicago, Illinois.

 What well-known Chicago airport is one of the busiest in the world?

 What is the name of the famous horse race held in Kentucky every May at Churchill Downs?

 The U.S. gold reserve is held at _____ in Kentucky.

 The _____ Aquarium in Chattanooga, Tennessee, is a popular tourist attraction known for its large fresh-water fish display.

Florida

Florida Everglades

Canton, Ohio

Michigan

Sears Tower

**Indianapolis
Motor Speedway**

Kentucky Derby

O Hare Airport

Tennessee

Fort Knox

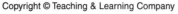

 Name the first national park in the United States.

 Yellowstone National Park is located in the states of Wyoming, Montana and _____.

 This national park has more geysers than anywhere on Earth.

 This geyser in Yellowstone National Park erupts on a regular schedule.

 Where is the largest U.S. national park located?

 Name the newest U.S. national park, which was added in 1999.

 _____ Tower in Wyoming became the first national monument in 1906.

 The "Great Register of the Desert" (Independence Rock) is a big boulder in Wyoming that early _____ carved or painted their names on as they headed west.

 The Continental Divide _____ throu_____ M_____

 Visitors to White Sands National Monument in New Mexico will see glistening white gypsum sand dunes that look like _____ fields.

Idaho

Yellowstone National Park

Old Faithful

Yellowstone National Park

Black Canyon of the Gunnison in Colorado

Wrangell-St. Elias National Park is in Alaska.

pioneers

Devils

snow

Rocky

 Visitors can see an amazing collection of rockets and space hardware at the U.S. Space and Rocket Center in what state?

 This Louisiana city is home to the Aquarium of the Americas.

 The climate-controlled Metrodome, which hosts baseball, football and basketball games, is located in what city and state?

 Visitors enjoy shopping and entertainment at the popular giant-sized Mall of America in Bloomington, _____.

 Fans of hot air balloons will enjoy the National Balloon Museum in Indianola in what state?

 This 630-foot tall, stainless steel structure was built in St. Louis, Missouri, to honor western pioneers.

 The St. Louis Gateway Arch is located on the banks of what river?

 This 90-mile stretch of rugged California coastline is known worldwide for its natural beauty.

 The International Peace Garden in North Dakota is a symbol of friendship and peace between the United States and what neighboring country?

 True or False? The tallest "structure" in the United States is a TV tower.

New Orleans

Alabama

Minnesota

Minneapolis, Minnesota

Gateway Arch

Iowa

Big Sur

Mississippi River

**True:
It is located in
Blanchard, North Dakota.**

Canada

Carlsbad Caverns National Park is home to over a hundred caves within the Guadalupe Mountains of what state?

Shoshone Falls in Idaho has been nicknamed the "Niagara of the _____."

Craters of the Moon National Monument and Preserve is located in what state: Utah or Idaho?

True or False? NASA astronauts practiced space missions at Idaho's Craters of the Moon National Monument and Preserve.

This Idaho river is nicknamed "The River of No Return."

Bryce Canyon National Park is famous for its beautiful canyons and cliffs. Is the park in Nevada or Utah?

The name of the world's largest natural arch, located in Utah is _____ .

Which one of the following tourist attractions is NOT in Utah: Zion National Park, Monument Valley, White Sands National Monument or Arches National Park?

Name the largest salt lake in North America.

True or False? The Great Salt Lake is 3-5 times saltier than the ocean.

West

New Mexico

true

Idaho

Utah

Salmon River

**White Sands
National Monument**

Rainbow Bridge

true

Great Salt Lake

 This South Dakota building is decorated with grain murals.

 Sixty-foot sculptures of four Presidents are carved into Mount Rushmore in what state?

 The faces of which four U.S. Presidents are sculpted into Mount Rushmore?

 How many years did it take to carve the Presidents' faces on Mount Rushmore National Memorial: 10 or 14?

 A large herd of _____ make their home at Custer State Park in South Dakota. This wild animal can weigh as much as 2000 pounds.

 The Lied Jungle in Omaha, Nebraska, has been called the world's largest indoor rain _____.

 Dwight D. Eisenhower's Presidental Library is located in Abilene in what state?

 True or False? Oil wells are located on the grounds of the Oklahoma state capitol building.

 What city is home to the National Cowboy Hall of Fame?

 The Johnson Space Center is located in what state?

South Dakota

Corn Palace

14 years

George Washington, Thomas Jefferson, Theodore Roosevelt, Abraham Lincoln

forest

bison

true

Kansas

Texas

Oklahoma City

 True or False?
The Great Salt
Lake used to be
a part of a large
freshwater lake.

 Which state is
nicknamed the
"Grand Canyon
State"?

 Name the
two main
rims of the
Grand Canyon.

 This body of
water links
Lake Erie to the
Hudson River.

 This national
park is
where George
Washington and
his soldiers
camped in 1777.

 The 277-mile-
long Grand
Canyon was
carved out by
what river?

 Grand Canyon
National Park is
home to many
animals. Name
the largest
carnivore that can
be found there.

 Petrified Forest
National Park
is located in
what state—
Arizona or
Nevada?

 Which tall
cactus has its
"own" national
park? Name
the cactus and
the park.

 The Sonoran
Desert is
located in
what two
countries?

Arizona

true

Erie Canal

**North Rim
and
South Rim**

Colorado River

**Valley Forge National
Historical Park**

Arizona

mountain lion

**United States
and Mexico**

**saguaro cactus;
Saguaro National Park**

 Name the historic mission in San Antonio, Texas, where a group of Texas soldiers fought several thousand Mexican soldiers.

 What is the name of the nation's largest ranch, which is located in Texas?

 Charles M. Russell was a famous western artist and sculptor. A collection of his work is on exhibit at the Charles M. Russell Museum in Great Falls. What state is it in?

 This national park in Wyoming includes Jackson Hole, glacial lakes and some of the youngest mountains in the world.

 Mesa Verde National Park in Colorado is known for its amazing _____.

 What is the most visited mountain in North America?

 True or False? Royal Gorge Bridge in Colorado is called the world's highest suspension bridge.

 Which of the U.S. military academies is located in Colorado Springs, Colorado?

 The Anasazi built four-story dwellings known as Pueblo Bonito in what western state?

 True or False? The Palace of the Governors built in 1610 in Santa Fe, New Mexico, is said to be the nation's oldest public building.

King Ranch

The Alamo

Grand Teton
National Park

Montana

Pikes Peak

cliff dwellings

U.S. Air Force
Academy

true

true

New Mexico

 In the Sonoran Desert lives a colorful lizard called a _____ monster.

 Meteor Crater is located in which state: Utah or Arizona?

 True or False? Colorado is nicknamed the "Silver State."

 The Valley of Fire in Nevada is known for its brilliant red _____.

 This California national park is home to the world's tallest living tree (385 feet tall).

 Fossils of animals and plants stuck in tar can be found at this popular California tourist attraction.

 The lowest point in the nation is _____ in California.

 The Mojave Desert is located in what western state?

 In what state is the San Andreas Fault located?

 The Cascade Mountain Range is located in the states of Washington, Oregon and _____.

Arizona

Gila

rocks

**False:
Nevada is the Silver State.**

La Brea Tar Pits

**Redwood
National Park**

California

Death Valley

California

California

 What is the largest Native American reservation in the United States?

 The Four Corners Monument was built to indicate where four states come together at one place. The four states are: Arizona, New Mexico, Utah and ____.

 Kitt Peak National Observatory in Arizona is famous for its large collection of ____.

 The Boulder Dam was renamed in 1947 to honor which U.S. President?

 The Golden Gate Bridge is one of the world's longest suspension bridges. In which state is this bridge located?

 This old prison located on an island in San Francisco Bay is a popular tourist attraction.

 Many tourists ride these unique vehicles to see the sites of San Francisco.

 Which migratory birds return every March to Mission San Juan Capistrano in California?

 What city is home to a tower called the Space Needle?

 The Space Needle was built in 1962 for the ____.

Colorado

Geography

Navajo Nation

Geography

Herbert Hoover

Geography

telescopes

Geography

Alcatraz

Geography

California

Geography

swallows

Geography

cable cars

Geography

World s Fair

Geography

Seattle, Washington

Geography

 Name the highest mountain in Oregon.

 What is the name of the deepest lake in the United States?

 True or False? Mount Saint Helens first erupted in the year 1960.

 This national forest in Alaska is the largest national forest in the United States.

 The highest mountain in North America is ____ located in Alaska.

 This island, nicknamed "Emerald Isle," is the largest island in Alaska.

 Hawaii has how many main islands?

 The Hawaiian Islands were created by ____.

 ____ is the well-known Hawaiian volcanic crater on the southeast coast of Oahu overlooking the Pacific Ocean.

 True or False? The nation's biggest active volcano is Mauna Loa, in Hawaii.

Crater Lake

Mt. Hood

Tongass National Forest

False: It first erupted in 1980.

Kodiak Island

Mount McKinley (in Denali National Park)

volcanoes

8

true

Diamond Head

 The Tacoma Totem Pole (105 feet tall) is one of the tallest in the Unitd States. Which state is it in?

 Which Washington State dam is the largest concrete structure in the United States?

 What river does the Grand Coulee Dam regulate: the Colorado River or the Columbia River?

 The statue that tops the Oregon State capitol honors the spirit of the state's early ____.

 This state is home to Sitka National Historical Park, which features a totem pole collection.

 The Trans-Alaska Pipeline System is used to move ____.

 What city is referred to as "The Big Apple"?

 This 10-story clock tower in Honolulu is a popular landmark and tourist attraction.

 The only royal palace in the United States is located in what state?

 This historic ranch on the Big Island of Hawaii is one of the oldest ranches in the United States.

Grand Coulee Dam

Washington

pioneers (or settlers)

Columbia River

oil

Alaska

Aloha Tower

New York City

Parker Ranch

Hawaii
It is Iolani Palace.

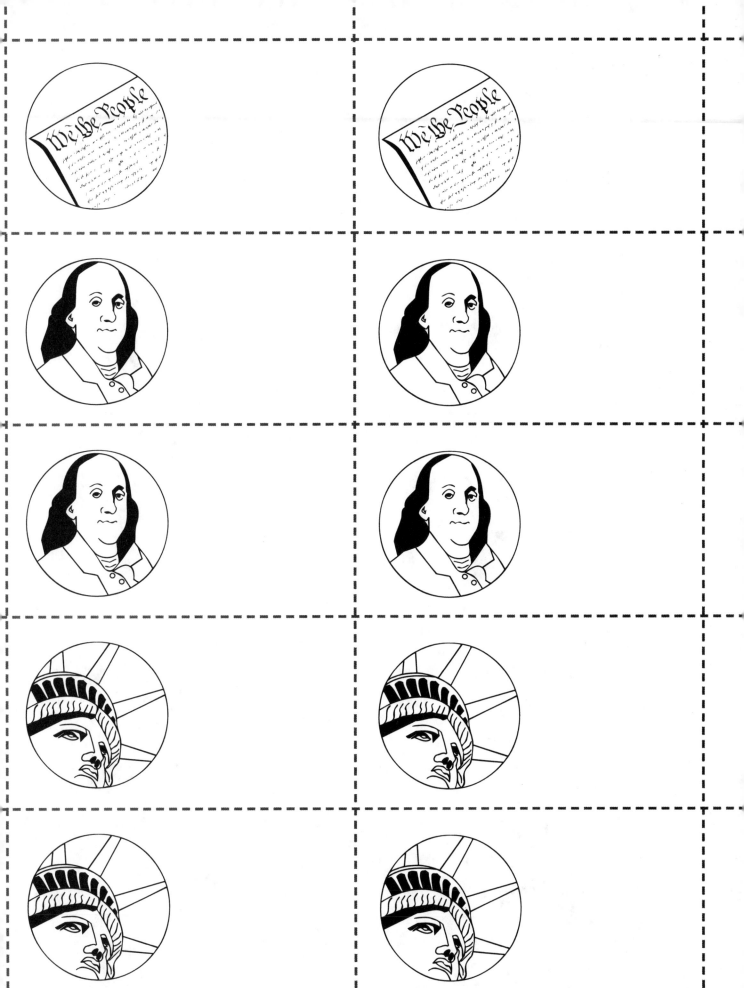